COUNTRY

Formal Name: Islamic Republic of Pakistan.

Short Form: Pakistan.

Term for Citizen(s): Pakistani(s).

Capital: Islamabad (Islamabad Capital Territory).

Major Cities: Pakistan has seven cities with a population
of 1 million or more: Karachi (9,339,023), Lahore (5,143,495),
Faisalabad (2,008,861), Rawalpindi (1,409,768), Multan
(1,197,384), Hyderabad (1,166,894), and Gujranwala (1,132,509).

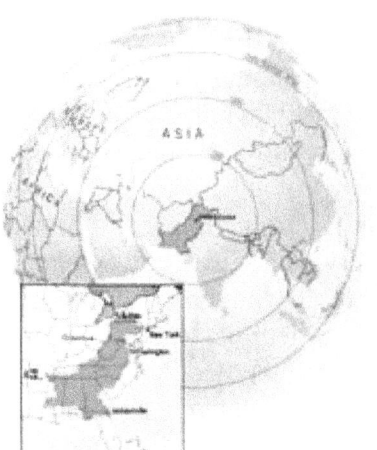
Click to Enlarge Image

Independence: Proclaimed August 14, 1947, from Britain.

Public Holidays: Eid-ul-Azha (Feast of the Sacrifice of Abraham, movable date); Muharram
(Islamic New Year, movable date); Kashmir Day (February 5); Ashura (movable date); Pakistan
Day (signing of first constitution and proclamation of the republic, March 23); Labour Day (May
1); Eid-i-Milad-un-Nabi (Birthday of the Prophet Muhammad, movable date); Independence Day
(August 14); Ramadan commencement (movable date); Iqbal Day (Birthday of Muhammad
Iqbal, November 9); Eid-ul-Fitr (end of Ramadan, movable date); Birthday of Quaid-i-Azam
Mohammad Ali Jinnah and Christmas (December 25). Muslim holidays are observed nationally,
and Christian holidays are elective for Christians only.

Flag:
Pakistan's flag is green with a narrow vertical white band on its left side.
A white crescent and star are in the center of the green band. Green
signifies the Muslim majority, white denotes minorities, the crescent
represents progress, and the star symbolizes light and knowledge.

Click to Enlarge Image

HISTORICAL BACKGROUND

Early Empires: Existing archaeological evidence suggests that humans lived in what became
Pakistan around 2.2 million years ago, and the first civilization in South Asia, the Harappan
Civilization, is believed to have started around 3000 B.C. in the Indus River valley. Indus
civilizations maintained irrigated agriculture, had contact with the Middle East and North Africa,
and endured until around 1750 B.C., when nomadic tribes from Central Asia called Aryans
conquered much of the Indus Valley. The Aryans maintained a system of social stratification

1

based on inherited occupation and physical separation of themselves from native peoples, and this system was justified religiously in scripts called Vedas that form the basis of Hinduism.

By 326 B.C., Chandra Gupta Maurya established the first empire in South Asia, but it was his grandson, Ashoka, who led the Mauryan Empire to political prominence around 200 B.C. In the following centuries, various powers exercised control in the subcontinent, although most only temporarily maintained dominance over particular regions. From A.D. 320–550, the Gupta Empire controlled much of the subcontinent with the assistance of locally based intermediaries.

Around 711, Arab general Muhammad bin Qasim introduced Islam into Sindh, and by the tenth century, Islam was further promoted by Turkish sultan Mahmud of Ghazni, who controlled Punjab. By the thirteenth century, a succession of Turkic rulers known as the Mughals ruled most of the Indian subcontinent, and their influence on architecture, cuisine, and language endures to the twenty-first century. However, Mughal rule eventually suffered from numerous difficulties related to controlling a large land area with distinct economies and cultures. One notable challenge to Mughal rule came from Sikh rulers who took control of the Punjabi capital Lahore in 1761. The Sikh ruler, Ranjit Singh, eventually controlled vast areas of Punjab by 1818 and Kashmir by 1819, but after Singh's death in 1840, infighting and factionalism among Sikh leaders led to the gradual disintegration of their holdings into small principalities. The British took advantage of the dissipation of Sikh power and ended Sikh rule by 1849.

European Influence: Although European contact with South Asia began in 1498 with the Portuguese, by the early 1800s the British had emerged as the preeminent political and economic power in much of the subcontinent. British dominance was far from complete, with at best tenuous control over what are now Pakistan's western provinces. The British East India Company initially administered most of the Indian subcontinent, but the Indian-led Sepoy Rebellion of 1857 seriously challenged British occupation and caused the British government to administer India directly. This near defeat for the British prompted changes in their administration of the subcontinent and in their attitudes toward Indians, particularly Muslims. Prior to 1857, Muslims were prominent in economics and administration, and Muslim leaders are believed to have led the Sepoy Rebellion to regain the political and economic advantages enjoyed under Mughal rule. The British responded by dropping Urdu and Persian as official languages and replacing them with English, thus rendering many Muslims functionally illiterate and unemployable. The British also placed Hindus in many positions previously occupied by Muslims. As a result, Muslims perceived Hindus as opportunistic accomplices to the British oppression of Muslims, and this impression would endure for decades.

Independence Movement: Muhammad Iqbal conceived the concept of a Muslim homeland called Pakistan ("Land of the Pure") in the 1920s, but the establishment of Pakistan was most advanced by Mohammad Ali Jinnah, a Bombay lawyer who proved to be a shrewd leader of the Muslim League political party. Jinnah claimed that India contained two nations, one Hindu and one Muslim, and that Muslims could not safely exist in a Hindu-dominated India. The degree to which Jinnah's objectives were motivated by religion is still debated, but his ideas resonated with Muslims who felt politically, economically, and socially discriminated against and with Muslims having theological interests in an Islamic state. At various times, the Muslim League acted independently of other groups and in shifting alliances with the colonial administration and the Congress Party of Mohandas Karamchand Gandhi. Nevertheless, its objective was always the establishment of an independent Muslim homeland.

World War II and widespread resistance to British rule in India created burdens that the British found too costly to bear, and in July 1947 the British announced their intention to withdraw from India. Pakistan was born as a bifurcated state in August 1947, divided by 1,600 kilometers of Indian soil and by economic and social divisions between a largely Bengali East Wing and a heavily Punjabi and Sindhi West Wing. The country also faced problems with absorbing millions of Muslim refugees from India, addressing substantial poverty, and establishing both a functioning government and a sense of national unity over a geographically and ethnically divided state. Just as daunting were the deficit of administrative personnel and limited material assets that curtailed the country's capacity to address its difficulties.

Post-Independence and Civil War: The influential founding fathers, Mohammad Ali Jinnah and Liaquat Ali Khan, had passed away by 1951, and their deaths were ominous precursors to the subsequent series of short-lived governments that changed just as often by military coup as by election. Pakistan was initially governed by a Constituent Assembly responsible for drafting a constitution and issuing legislation until the constitution went into force. However, the constitution's drafting was delayed by disagreements over how different regions would be represented and how the state would embody Islamic principles. Legislative paralysis prompted Governor General Ghulam Mohammad to dismiss the Constituent Assembly in 1954. This action is now seen as the beginning of "viceregal" politics in Pakistan, in which the military and civil bureaucracy, not elected officials, govern the country and maintain substantial influence over society and the provinces. A new Constituent Assembly wrote the first constitution in 1956 and reconstituted itself as the Legislative Assembly. However, regional rivalries between East and West Pakistan and ethnic and religious tensions threatened political stability, and on October 7, 1958, President Iskander Mirza disbanded the Legislative Assembly. Later that month, Mirza himself was overthrown by General Mohammad Ayub Khan.

Ayub Khan saw himself as a reformer who would bring much-needed stability to the country, and he started by establishing a system of local governments called Basic Democracies for communities to have meaningful input into politics. But Ayub quickly lost interest and turned toward the civil bureaucracy for policy advice and formation. A new constitution was promulgated in 1962, and it established a weak legislature (the National Assembly) and a president with substantial legislative, executive, and financial powers.

Possibly the most notable event of Ayub's tenure was a 17-day war with India in 1965 over the nagging Kashmir dispute. Pakistan argued that under the terms of the 1947 partition, Muslim-dominant areas of the subcontinent should become part of Pakistan and claimed that India had pressured the Hindu ruler of Kashmir to accede to India at the time of partition, ostensibly against the wishes of the largely Muslim population. The 1965 war had the unintended consequences of interrupting impressive economic growth and deflating the military's confidence in its own abilities. Amid worsening societal and political problems, substantial popular opposition, and his own declining health, Ayub Khan resigned in 1969.

Subsequently, General Agha Mohammad Yahya Khan became president and chief martial law administrator, and he attempted to reinstitute parliamentary democracy. However, festering tensions over representation in the National Assembly led to civil war between East and West Pakistan in 1971. With Indian assistance, East Pakistan seceded and became the independent nation of Bangladesh. At the same time, India and West Pakistan fought another 17-day war, mostly in West Pakistan, which ended in a cease-fire agreement. Largely as a result of Pakistan's military losses, Yahya resigned in 1971, and Zulfiqar Ali Bhutto was appointed president, becoming the first civilian head of government in nearly two decades.

Emergence of Civilian Rule: Bhutto lifted martial law, and a new constitution came into effect in August 1973. The constitution was heavily concerned with the role of Islam, the distribution of power between the federal and provincial governments, and the division of responsibilities between the president and prime minister, the latter assuming greater authority than before. Bhutto nationalized numerous industries, and the government's heavy involvement in the economy would have enduring economic repercussions. The country appeared to be democratizing, but political opposition grew against Bhutto's repression of political opponents and alleged voting irregularities. In July 1977, Bhutto was overthrown, and General Mohammad Zia ul-Haq became chief martial law administrator. Bhutto eventually was sentenced to death on charges of conspiring to murder a political opponent and was executed in 1979.

Martial Law and Islamization: Zia adapted the structure of Ayub Khan's Basic Democracies to a new system of local governments and also adopted various measures to create an Islamic state. When the Soviet Union invaded Afghanistan in 1979, Pakistan became the recipient of numerous Afghan refugees and large-scale foreign aid from the United States, China, Saudi Arabia, and others. The refugees and financial assistance continued until the war's end in 1989.

Zia officially terminated martial law in 1985 by assuming the presidency and reinstating the 1973 constitution. However, he also added the Eighth Amendment, which empowered the president to appoint and dismiss the prime minister and provincial governors and to dissolve the national and provincial legislatures. When Zia died in an airplane crash in August 1988, Benazir Bhutto—head of the Pakistan People's Party (PPP) and daughter of Zulfiqar Ali Bhutto—became prime minister. Pakistan thus became the first Muslim country with a female head of government.

The Restoration of Civilian Government: Bhutto's government was plagued by ethnic conflict, severe economic problems, and a lack of legislative support. In October 1990, Mian Nawaz Sharif, leader of the Islamic Democratic Alliance (IDA), became prime minister and faced the same problems that troubled Bhutto. In 1993 Bhutto's PPP won the National Assembly, and she once again became prime minister. However, in 1996 President Farooq Leghari dismissed Bhutto on charges of corruption, and in 1997 Nawaz Sharif replaced her.

In 1998 India conducted nuclear tests, and two weeks later Pakistan reacted by detonating five nuclear devices. Many countries responded with condemnation and sanctions, but Pakistan felt that it finally possessed sufficient deterrent force against its perennial rival, India. Deterrence failed to hold, however, and in October 1999 India and Pakistan engaged in a limited conflict (the Kargil War), which Pakistan was widely seen as precipitating because of its suspected support of militants who entered Indian-held Kashmir from Pakistani-held Kashmir. The conflict proved to be embarrassing for the government, and, with the economy suffering tremendously, General Pervez Musharraf overthrew Nawaz Sharif in late October 1999.

Return to Military Rule: Musharraf became both president and chief of army staff, and he further consolidated his power through various legal measures. After the September 11, 2001, terrorist attacks in the United States, Musharraf's government benefited from an infusion of economic and military aid, because Pakistan is seen as an important ally in the war on terrorism. However, Pakistan was widely suspected of complicity in a terrorist attack on India's parliament in December 2001. In an April 2002 national referendum, Musharraf's tenure as president was extended to 2007. In late 2004, Musharraf reneged on a previous commitment to relinquish his position as chief of army staff, much to the chagrin of many secular and religious political parties, who demanded that elections be held in early 2005.

In 2005 Pakistan continued to face many of the same problems that have plagued the country since its inception: government instability, tense relations with India, ethnic tensions, political divisions among provinces, economic dependence on international aid, and weak prospects for democracy. However, Pakistan's government continued to survive and society to endure in spite of such difficulties, occasionally exhibiting remarkable flexibility and resilience. Indeed, it is often difficult to tell if Pakistan is on the precipice of disintegration or on the verge of renewal.

GEOGRAPHY

Click to Enlarge Image

Location: Located in South Asia, Pakistan borders Iran to the southwest, Afghanistan to the west and north, China to the northeast, and India to the east. The Arabian Sea marks Pakistan's southern boundary.

Size: Pakistan's exact size is debated because of its disputed border with India. According to the United Nations and the Pakistan government, the country has a total area of 796,095 square kilometers. This figure, however, does not include the Pakistan-administered portions of Jammu and Kashmir (known as Azad Kashmir and the Northern Areas, with areas of 11,639 square kilometers and 72,520 square kilometers, respectively). These areas are claimed by Pakistan, but because their possession is disputed, they are not included in official land area statistics.

Land Boundaries: Pakistan shares borders with Afghanistan (2,430 kilometers), China (523 kilometers), India (2,912 kilometers), and Iran (909 kilometers).

Disputed Territory: Afghanistan disputes the legitimacy of its border with Pakistan, and at times Afghanistan's governments have argued that all Pashtun (Pakhtun) territory in Afghanistan and Pakistan should be under Afghan control. Pakistan and India have disputed possession of Jammu and Kashmir since 1947, and the issue remains unresolved despite numerous cease-fire agreements between the two countries. Jammu and Kashmir is split between the two countries by a United Nations-monitored border called the Line of Control.

Length of Coastline: Pakistan's coastline totals 1,064 kilometers along the Arabian Sea.

Maritime Claims: Under the 1982 United Nations Convention on the Law of the Sea, Pakistan claims a 200-nautical-mile exclusive economic zone, a 12-nautical-mile territorial sea, and a 24-nautical-mile contiguous zone for security, immigration, customs, and other matters.

Topography: Pakistan has a diverse array of landscapes spread among nine major ecological zones. Its territory encompasses portions of the Himalaya, Hindu Kush, and Karakoram mountain ranges, making it home to some of the world's highest mountains, including K2, which at 8,611 meters above sea level is the world's second highest peak. Intermountain valleys make up much of the North-West Frontier Province, and rugged plateaus cover much of Balochistan Province in the west. In the east, expansive, irrigated plains along the Indus River cover much of of Punjab and Sindh provinces, which have deserts as well (Cholistan in Punjab, Thar in Sindh).

Principal Rivers: The main rivers are the Indus (2,749 kilometers within Pakistan) and its tributaries: the Chenab (730.6 kilometers), Ravi (680.6 kilometers), Jhelum (611.3 kilometers), and Sutlej (530.6 kilometers). The navigable portions of these rivers are generally small and unconnected as a result of seasonal variations in water flows and the presence of substantial irrigation structures.

Climate: Most of Pakistan has a generally dry climate and receives less than 250 millimeters of rain per year, although northern and southern areas have noticeable climatic differences. The average annual temperature is around 27°C, but temperatures vary with elevation from –30°C to –10°C during the coldest months in mountainous and northern areas of Pakistan-administered Kashmir to 50°C in the warmest months in parts of Punjab, Sindh, and the Balochistan Plateau. Mid-December to March is dry and cool; April to June is hot, with 25 to 50 percent relative humidity; July to September is the wet monsoon season; and October-November is the dry post-monsoon season, with hot temperatures nationwide.

Natural Resources: Economically important natural resources include arable land, chromite, coal, copper, fireclay, gypsum, iron, limestone, oil, natural gas, rock salt, and silica sand.

Land Use: More than 40 percent of the working population is employed in agriculture, yet the per capita amount of agricultural land is declining, and there are significant natural limitations to increasing the quantity of arable land. According to official statistics for 2004, the country's total land area is 79.6 million hectares, but only 59.3 million hectares have been surveyed. Out of the surveyed land area, 24.6 million hectares are classified as not available for cultivation, 3.6 million hectares are forest area, and 9.2 million hectares are unused but believed to be cultivable. Approximately 22 million hectares are used for cultivation, of which nearly 16 million hectares are actually sown, with the remainder left fallow. About 13.5 million hectares of the sown area are irrigated, and 6.5 million hectares are sown more than once per year. Most cultivable and irrigated land is located in the eastern provinces of Punjab and Sindh around the Indus River and its tributaries. Pakistan has an extensive but inefficient canal system for irrigation, and much of the crop area is rain fed, but precipitation tends to be unevenly distributed throughout the year.

Environmental Factors: Numerous environmental problems threaten the economy and the population's health, and there is little indication of their abatement. A 1997 World Bank study estimated the annual cost of Pakistan's environmental problems at US$1.8 billion in health expenditures, reduced labor productivity, and other costs. The availability of natural resources is limited by the dry climate and mountainous terrain, substantial population growth is increasing pressure on the resource base, and resource management has suffered from the emphasis on rapid economic growth and often-unregulated forms of economic productivity. As a result, human transformation of the environment is manifest in several problems. Population growth and poor water infrastructure have reduced per capita water availability from 53,000 cubic meters to 1,200 cubic meters, and heavy reliance on firewood has contributed to the world's second highest rate of deforestation. Poor agricultural practices have led to soil erosion, groundwater degradation, and other problems that have hindered crop output and contributed to health problems for rural communities. Solid waste burning, low-quality fuels, and the growing use of fuel-inefficient motor vehicles have contributed to air pollution that in some cities—such as Islamabad, Lahore, and Rawalpindi—has exceeded levels deemed safe by the World Health Organization.

The government has expressed concern about environmental threats to economic growth and social development and, since the early 1990s, has addressed environmental concerns with new legislation and institutions such as the Pakistan Environment Protection Council. Yet, foreign lenders provide most environmental protection funds, and only 0.04 percent of the government's development budget goes to environmental protection. Thus, the government's ability to enforce environmental regulations is limited, and private industries often lack funds to meet environmental standards established by international trade organizations.

Time Zone: Pakistan is in a single time zone, Greenwich Mean Time plus 5.5 hours.

SOCIETY

Population: Pakistan has a large, mostly rural population with a high rate of growth. The government estimates the population at 152.8 million as of December 2004, not including 1.2 million refugees from Afghanistan (2002 estimate). From 1981 to 1998, population growth averaged nearly 2.7 percent annually. If this growth rate continues, the population will double approximately every 26 years. According to Pakistan's 1998 census, the overall population density was 166.3 persons per square kilometer, but provincial population densities range from 18.9 in Balochistan to 358.5 in Punjab. Furthermore, the population is clustered in the eastern provinces of Punjab and Sindh, which contain 78.6 percent of the total population. According to the 1998 census, 67.5 percent of the population lived in rural areas. Only Sindh had roughly equal rural and urban populations (51.2 percent and 48.8 percent, respectively).

Demography: Pakistan's fast-growing population has a substantial proportion of youths. In 2004, 40.2 percent of the population was aged 14 or younger, 55.7 percent was 15–64 years of age, and only 4.1 percent of the population was 65 and older. According to Pakistan government statistics, 52 percent of the population is male. In 2000 Pakistan's crude birthrate was 29.1 births per 1,000, and the total fertility rate was 4.3 births per woman. The infant mortality rate was 79.8 deaths per 1,000 live births, and the crude death rate was 7.8 deaths per 1,000. Life expectancy at birth was 64 years for males and 66 years for females.

Ethnic Groups: Ethnic groups in Pakistan generally are categorized according to various combinations of religion, language, and sometimes tribe. Punjabis are the largest linguistic group (44.2 percent of the population) and often are divided into three occupational castes: Rajputs, Jats, and Arains. Pakhtuns (15.4 percent) are the dominant ethnic group in the North-West Frontier Province, but Pakhtuns belong to different tribes or kinship groups and have no central governing authority. Sindhis (14.1 percent) are dominant in Sindh and are divided into occupational and caste groupings. Balochis (3.6 percent) are dominant in Balochistan and are divided into various eastern and western tribes. Other ethnolinguistic groups include the Siraikis, who live mostly in Punjab; Urdu-speaking Muhajirs, refugees from India and their descendants who migrated to Pakistan during the 1947 partition and are concentrated in Sindh; and Brahuis, a Dravidian language group in Sindh and Balochistan.

Languages: Urdu is the national language and the language of most print media. English has official status and often is regarded as the language of the elite and upwardly mobile. Urdu and English often are used in government and business. Punjabi is the most common language, spoken by 44.2 percent of the population, followed by Pakhtu (15.2 percent), Sindhi (14.1 percent), Siraiki (10.5 percent), Urdu (7.8 percent), and Balochi (3.8 percent). Smaller linguistic groups include the Hindko in the North-West Frontier Province, the Farsi-speaking Hazaras of Balochistan, and the Brahuis in Sindh and Balochistan. Language often articulates ethnic identity, and provincial boundaries are linguistically based. Urdu has been promoted as a means of unifying ethnic groups, but it is the mother tongue of only the Muhajirs. Furthermore, many groups perceive the establishment of Urdu as the national language as threatening to their employment potential, political participation, and ethnic identity.

Religion: The overwhelming majority of the population (96.3 percent) is Muslim, of whom approximately 95 percent are Sunni and 5 percent Shia. Sunnis and Shias are subdivided into numerous sects. Approximately 1.6 percent of the population is Hindu, 1.6 percent is Christian, and 0.3 percent belongs to other religions, such as Bahaism and Sikhism. Some 0.2 percent of the population is Ahmadiyya (also known as Qadiani), a small but influential sect that maintains some Islamic beliefs but is considered heretical by orthodox Muslims and is not recognized as Muslim by Pakistani law.

The country was founded to promote religious freedom, and the constitution guarantees freedom of religion. However, Islam is the state religion, and the constitution states that religious practice is "subject to law, public order, and morality." The government also has Islamic institutions such as the Federal Shariat Court and the Council of Islamic Ideology, which advise politicians on the congruence of legislation with Islamic injunctions. It is debatable whether the government has established such institutions for religious or political reasons, but the government has promoted Islam as a means of unifying numerous ethnic groups. Nevertheless, political, economic, and religious differences have been manifested in occasionally violent conflicts between religious communities, particularly between Sunni and Shia militias.

Education and Literacy: Pakistan has low indicators of educational attainment, and education has been underfunded for decades. According to the 1998 census, 43.9 percent of those aged 10 or older were literate, but the literacy rate was higher for males (54.8 percent) than for females (32.0 percent). The 2003 estimates for literacy were 45.7 percent for those 15 years of age and older (59.8 percent for males and 30.6 percent for females). The country's enrollment rate for those aged 5 to 24 is 36 percent (41.2 percent for males, 30.4 percent for females), and literacy and enrollment rates tend to be higher in urban areas. In 2001 the government announced plans to institute universal primary education by 2010 and 78 percent literacy by 2011. However, more than 50 percent of the funds for this initiative are expected to come from international donors. During the 1980s and most of the 1990s, public expenditures on education averaged 2.5 percent of gross domestic product (GDP), but have fallen to less than 2 percent of GDP since 1998. Of the fiscal year (FY) 2004 budget's current expenditures, US$161.1 million—1.4 percent—was allocated to education, as was US$201.6 million—1.7 percent—of the FY 2005 budget.

Free primary education is a constitutional right and is compulsory in every province except Balochistan. The education system is designed for 12 years of schooling, with five years in primary school, three in middle school, and four in high school. According to 2001 government figures, the system included 147,736 primary schools, 25,472 middle-level schools, 15,416 high schools and vocational institutions, 352 professional colleges, and 26 universities. In addition to public and private schools, an indeterminate number of mosque-administered madrassas provide free room, board, and theological education, which makes them an attractive option for poor families. Some madrassas are suspected of having links to religious militants, prompting the government to announce its intention of establishing greater regulation over these institutions.

Health: Pakistan's health indicators, health funding, and health and sanitation infrastructure are generally poor, particularly in rural areas. About 19 percent of the population is malnourished—a higher rate than the 17 percent average for developing countries—and 30 percent of children under age five are malnourished. Leading causes of sickness and death include gastroenteritis, respiratory infections, congenital abnormalities, tuberculosis, malaria, and typhoid fever. The United Nations estimates that in 2003 Pakistan's human immunodeficiency virus (HIV) prevalence rate was 0.1 percent among those 15–49, with an estimated 4,900 deaths from acquired immune deficiency syndrome (AIDS). AIDS is a major health concern, and both the government and religious community are engaging in efforts to reduce its spread.

In 2003 there were 68 physicians for every 100,000 persons in Pakistan. According to 2002 government statistics, there were 12,501 health institutions nationwide, including 4,590 dispensaries, 906 hospitals with a total of 80,665 hospital beds, and 550 rural health centers with a total of 8,840 beds. According to the World Health Organization, Pakistan's total health expenditures amounted to 3.9 percent of gross domestic product (GDP) in 2001, and per capita health expenditures were US$16. The government provided 24.4 percent of total health expenditures, with the remainder being entirely private, out-of-pocket expenses.

Welfare: Indicators for education, health, and some other aspects of human development have improved since the early 1990s. According to Pakistan's Ministry of Finance, government expenditures for the social sector and poverty reduction totaled roughly US$14.6 billion from fiscal year (FY) 2000 to FY 2004. Nevertheless, poverty increased in the late 1990s, and the country's population growth reduced income growth. The proportion of the population living below the poverty line increased from 34 percent in 1991 to 44 percent by 2002, reversing decades of decline. Social service funding and institutions are inadequate to address the development problems faced by much of the Pakistani population. Provincial governments are responsible for providing social services but often lack the financial and institutional resources to do so. Most social services funding comes from the federal government and international aid, but corruption and institutional inefficiencies have hindered programs designed to alleviate unemployment, poverty, and other social ills. Furthermore, the economic, political, and educational opportunities of women and religious minorities have been limited by persistent discrimination in both government and society.

ECONOMY

Overview: Throughout the 1990s, Pakistan's economy suffered for a number of reasons, but from 2002 to 2004 the economy has recovered as a result of changes in government policies and the resumption of international lending. Economic statistics do not reflect the reality of the economy, because official economic data omit the informal economy, which is estimated to equal about 30 percent of the formal economy. Agriculture employs the greatest proportion of the working population but accounts for less than 25 percent of gross domestic product (GDP). This discrepancy is the result of rapid growth in services and industry since the 1980s, although major industries, such as textiles and sugar, are heavily reliant on agriculture.

Since independence, economic growth rates have been impressive but also have fluctuated widely. These fluctuations have occurred largely because successive governments have emphasized different sectors through changes in subsidies, regulations, and state ownership of industry. Furthermore, shifts in international aid and foreign capital flows have influenced economic growth through changes in government spending and budget deficits. Still, from 2002 to 2004 there were surpluses in the current account, inflation was low, and export growth was the highest in almost a decade.

Economic liberalization and deregulation began in the early 1980s, continued through the 1990s, and have accelerated under the government of President Pervez Musharraf (1999–). The government has shifted from state ownership of many industries and heavy regulation of the private economy to privatization of some state industries, deregulation, facilitation of capital flows, and reforms of the financial system and monetary policy. Still, lax fiscal and monetary policies, infrastructural deficiencies, a poorly developed human resource base, and persistent market distortions that benefit a small elite of landowners, industrialists, and others undercut economic potential.

Gross Domestic Product (GDP)/Power Purchasing Parity (PPP): According to World Bank data, in 2003 Pakistan's GDP was US$68.6 billion, gross national income (GNI) per capita was US$430, and PPP per capita was US$2,060. GDP grew an average of 5.4 percent annually from 1961 to 2003, but average annual GDP growth from 1993 to 2003 was lower, at 3.4 percent. Similarly, per capita GDP grew at an annual average of 2.6 percent from 1961 to 2003 and 0.9 percent from 1993 to 2003. From 1974 to 2004, agriculture's proportion of GDP declined from

35 to 23 percent, whereas the proportion created by services increased from 43 percent to 52 percent, and industry and manufacturing increased slightly from 22 percent to 25 percent.

Government Budget: In fiscal year (FY) 2004, Pakistan's total expenditures were US$16.0 billion, and total revenues were US$13.1 billion, both higher than in previous years. The federal budget has two components: the development budget for capital investment and development programs and the ordinary budget covering current expenditures such as defense and debt servicing. In FY 2004 current expenditures accounted for 82.9 percent of total expenditures. Debt servicing accounted for 21.1 percent of overall expenditures, defense for 18.0 percent, and development programs for 15.9 percent. During the 1990s and early 2000s, current expenditures were approximately 80 percent of planned spending, with debt servicing and defense accounting, respectively, for 35 percent and 25 percent of all expenditures. Provinces have their own budgets and limited tax powers, but about 25 percent of the federal budget is distributed to provincial governments to provide agricultural and social services.

From 1993 to 2003, the budget deficit declined, from 8.1 to 4.5 percent of gross domestic product (GDP), and current revenues increased, from 18.1 to 20.8 percent of GDP. Historically, tax collection has been extremely poor as a result of the corrupt, poorly functioning tax administration and numerous tax exemptions. In the 1990s, an estimated 80 percent of tax revenues came from indirect sources, and only 1.1 million of the country's approximately 130 million people were on the tax rolls. However, from 1999 to 2004 the government instituted several tax reforms that reduced some tax exemptions, decreased excise taxes, and lowered tax rates for banks and private limited companies.

Inflation: The exact figures for inflation rates vary by source, but it is clear that rates of inflation declined throughout the 1990s and early 2000s. According to World Bank figures, inflation peaked at 25 percent in 1974, ranged from approximately 4 percent to 11 percent in the late 1970s and 1980s, and rose to 13 percent in 1991. After 1991, inflation generally declined to 2.4 percent in 2002 and 4.2 percent in 2003.

Agriculture, Forestry, and Fishing: According to official sources, agriculture, livestock, fishing, and forestry produced an estimated 23.3 percent of gross domestic product (GDP) for FY 2004. Employment in this sector has declined as other economic sectors have grown. Approximately 43.1 percent of the working population was employed in agriculture, forestry, and fishing in 2002, down from 48.3 percent in 1992, but still the largest proportion of the workforce among all economic sectors.

The major crops are wheat, rice, sugarcane, and cotton. Because of the generally arid climate and low soil moisture, agricultural production relies heavily on irrigation, nearly all of which is found in the east, around the Indus River and its tributaries. Agricultural growth has averaged around 4 percent annually since independence, and from 1947 to 2003 total food crop production increased from 4.7 million tons to 25.9 million tons. Substantial agricultural growth began in the 1960s with the use of high-yielding crops, increased government prices for crops, and subsidies for irrigation water, fertilizer, and other inputs. By the 1980s, Pakistan had become a net exporter of food grains. However, by the 1990s cotton output had declined, and the country became a net importer of food grains as the rate of population growth continued to exceed the rate of agricultural growth. The country's unfulfilled agricultural potential is often seen as the result of the domination of large landowners, deterioration in the irrigation network, soil degradation from fertilizers, and poor government investment in agricultural research.

Mining and Minerals: Mining and minerals historically have been a weak economic sector. Since 2000 mining and quarrying have accounted annually for around 1.4 percent of gross domestic product (GDP) and employed an estimated 0.1 percent of the working population. Chromite is the only metallic ore that has been exploited on a commercial scale, but the country has substantial deposits of copper and iron ores as well. Pakistan also has significant deposits of non-metallic ores such as anhydrite, dolomite, gypsum, limestone, marble, and rock salt.

Industry and Manufacturing: Since the mid-1960s, the industrial sector has produced 19 to 25 percent of gross domestic product (GDP), accounting for 24.5 percent of GDP in 2004. Manufacturing and construction dominate the industrial sector, accounting for around 19 percent of GDP. Since the 1980s, approximately 17 to 20 percent of the working population has been employed in the industrial sector (25 percent in 2004), mostly in manufacturing and construction. Although the industrial base has diversified since independence, the production base depends heavily on textiles and sugar. Manufacturing output is therefore vulnerable to adverse weather conditions and fluctuations in international prices for cotton and sugar. Various liberalization reforms have been pursued since the early 1980s but have been hindered by substantial corruption, frequent raw material shortages, the government's tendency to provide generous concessions to particular sectors (such as sugar refining and yarn spinning), and a burdensome tax structure that has helped promote the development of the informal economy.

Energy: Economic growth, population growth, and rising urbanization have increased energy demand, much of which is met by imported energy sources because of the country's limited domestic energy resources. Traditional resources, such as firewood and dung, are commonly used, particularly in rural areas, and the government plans to reduce firewood consumption by introducing solar power to rural areas. Coal has provided around 5 percent of total domestic energy supply for decades, but most is of poor quality and generally is used in brick kilns.

With regard to nontraditional sources, oil and natural gas have provided around 37 to 43 percent of total energy supplies each since the late 1970s, and the country is attempting to expand hydropower production. For decades, Pakistan has depended heavily on oil imports, and in FY 2003 imported oil provided 31.6 percent of total energy supplies—at a cost of US$3.1 billion. Domestic oil provided 6.7 percent of total energy supplies, and domestic recoverable petroleum reserves have fallen to less than 50 percent of their estimated original amount. However, natural gas production nearly doubled to 2.7 million cubic feet per day in FY 2003, providing 43.8 percent of the total energy supply. The government has considered pipelines that could import around 1.5 billion cubic feet of gas per day, but as of early 2005 these plans were still under review. Hydropower has declined from 17.7 percent of total energy supply in FY 1979 to 11.3 percent in FY 2003. The government is interested in reversing this trend, but the area with the greatest potential for hydropower expansion (the mountainous north) is difficult to access and would have high transmission costs. Finally, nuclear power production was meager until the 2001 inauguration of the country's second nuclear power facility, and nuclear energy production increased to 1.2 percent of total energy supply in FY 2003.

Services: The services sector accounts for about 50 percent of Pakistan's annual gross domestic product (GDP). From 2000 to 2004, transportation, wholesale and retail trade, finance, public administration, defense, and services collectively provided about 52 percent of GDP. Services alone were about 9 to 10 percent of GDP. The services sector has suffered from many of the same problems as the industrial sector, such as political corruption and crippling tax rates, and sectoral growth has been limited by a dearth of educational resources and skilled labor.

Banking and Finance: Multilateral creditors have been a major source of finance and a major influence on economic and social development policies. However, bilateral and multilateral creditors periodically have ceased lending for economic reasons, such as government unwillingness or inability to comply with loan conditions, or political reasons, such as the 1998 nuclear tests and the 1999 military coup. Loans generally have resumed after the government agrees to loan conditions or internationally influential countries reduce their opposition to continued loans. In spite of inexpensive labor, a large domestic market, and access to regional markets, investors often are repelled by corruption, infrastructural difficulties, and various law and order problems in Pakistan. The government has pursued various reforms and liberalization measures, but domestic opposition has weakened implementation.

Domestic banking suffered in the 1990s but has shown signs of improvement from 2002 to 2004. In the 1990s, the government borrowed heavily from the domestic banking system, which prevented interest rates from declining and contributed to growth in the money supply and subsequent inflation. In addition, major domestic manufacturers failed to honor debts to domestic banks. However, from 2002 to 2004 privatization and deregulation of oil, gas, communications, and finance led to increases in investment. Overall investment in the early 1990s was around 19 percent of gross domestic product (GDP) annually but fell to 14.7 percent of GDP by FY 2001 and then increased to 15.5 percent of GDP by FY 2003.

Tourism: According to government statistics, the number of foreign tourists declined throughout the 1990s, as did earnings from foreign tourism. The number of foreign tourists ranged from 80,000 to 180,000 from the mid-1980s to the mid-1990s but dropped to around 70,000 annually thereafter. Pakistan receives about 6 percent of the foreign tourists who visit South Asia. Foreign exchange receipts from tourists peaked at US$156.5 million in 1990 but dropped to US$117 million by the end of the 1990s. The decline in foreign tourists is believed to be due to security concerns and lack of government effort to attract tourists.

Labor: Labor figures are difficult to assess, partly because of the large number of workers in the informal economy. According to government statistics for FY 2004, 30.4 percent of the total population is in the official, civilian labor force, with 28.1 percent classified as employed and 2.3 percent categorized as unemployed. Other figures put the unemployment rate at around 19.7 percent. A much greater percentage of men (83.1 percent) than women (16.9 percent) are active in the official civilian labor force. Agriculture, forestry, and fishing employ the greatest proportion of the civilian labor force (43.1 percent), followed by "community, social, and personal services" (15 percent), wholesale and retail trade (14.8 percent), and manufacturing (13.7 percent). These percentages have changed little since the 1960s. However, the informal economy employs the majority of workers—about 70 percent according to government data from

1974 to 2004—with most employed in wholesale and retail trade, manufacturing, or "community, social, and personal services." Child labor is regarded as a prevalent problem. Although the exact number of child laborers is not known, official data indicate that 12.8 percent of those 10 to 14 years of age are active in the official labor force.

Foreign Economic Relations: Pakistan is a member of the Asian Development Bank (ADB), the Colombo Plan, the South Asian Association for Regional Cooperation (SAARC), and the United Nations Economic and Social Commission for Asia and the Pacific (ESCAP). It has free-trade arrangements (FTAs) with China, Sri Lanka, and the European Union, and by the end of 2004 had sought FTAs with Mexico and the United States. Historically, political issues have affected Pakistan's foreign trade and aid. In 1998 the United States and international donors imposed sanctions because of Pakistan's successful nuclear tests. Those sanctions were dropped after the September 11, 2001, terrorist attacks because the United States regarded Pakistan as an important ally against transnational terrorists operating out of Afghanistan.

Imports: In 2003 imports totaled US$11.3 billion, up from around US$1.2 billion in the late 1960s. Imports of goods and services have constituted about 20 percent of gross domestic product (GDP) since the late 1960s, and since the early 1990s machinery, petroleum products, and chemicals have composed around 55 percent of imported goods. Most imports come from the United States, Japan, Kuwait, Saudi Arabia, Germany, the United Kingdom, and Malaysia. Imports increased throughout the 1990s, at least partly because the government reduced maximum tariff rates from 92 percent in 1994 to 35 percent in 1999.

Exports: In 2003 exports of goods and services totaled US$10.9 billion, up from around US$750 million in the late 1960s. Exports of goods and services have increased from around 10 percent of gross domestic product (GDP) in the late 1960s to 15 percent throughout the 1990s. Since the early 1990s, primary commodity exports have fallen from about 20 percent to 10 percent of exports, while manufactured goods have increased from 55 percent to 75 percent. Manufactured cotton textiles have accounted for about 60 percent of total exports since the early 1990s, and other manufactured goods (such as leather goods, pharmaceuticals, and sporting goods) and primary commodities (particularly rice) for 25 percent of exports. The primary importers of Pakistani goods are the United States, Germany, Japan, the United Kingdom, Hong Kong, the United Arab Emirates, and Saudi Arabia. Since 2000, Pakistan has promoted exports by rebating import duties, sales taxes, and income taxes, and by concessional export financing.

Trade Balance: Pakistan has had an annual trade deficit since the early 1970s. According to government data, the trade deficit in goods was US$1.5 billion in FY 1991, increased to US$3.7 billion in FY 1997, and thereafter declined to US$1.1 billion in FY 2003. A similar trend is evident in World Bank figures for Pakistan's external balance on goods and services, with a deficit of US$691 million in 1970, US$3.1 billion in 1990, and US$444 million in 2003.

Balance of Payments: Data vary by source, and from 1993 to 2004 government institutions did not report relevant statistics according to International Monetary Fund guidelines for member states. However, it is clear that Pakistan has had balance of payments difficulties for decades, largely as a result of current account deficits ranging from US$750 million to US$2.7 billion from 1970 to 2001. Historically, current account deficits have been due to trade deficits.

14

However, from 2002 to 2004 current account surpluses ranged from US$1.9 billion to US$4.2 billion as trade deficits declined and private transfers increased—particularly remittances from Pakistanis working outside the country. As a result of balance of payments problems, the official currency, the rupee, often has declined in value, and the government frequently has had to reschedule debt payments and resort to high-interest emergency borrowing.

External Debt: Estimates of the size of Pakistan's external debt vary by source. However, observers generally believe that the combination of poor tax administration, high government expenditures, and heavy dependence on external funds has resulted in massive fiscal deficits that, at times, have nearly crippled the economy and rendered Pakistan one of the world's most indebted countries. When the United States and international lending agencies imposed sanctions after Pakistan's 1998 nuclear tests, the country was close to defaulting on external obligations. According to the World Bank and the State Bank of Pakistan, Pakistan's total external debt was approximately US$3.4 billion in 1970, US$9.9 billion in 1980, US$20.6 billion in 1990, and US$36.1 billion in 2003 (about 52.6 percent of the gross domestic product).

Foreign Investment: Since the 1980s, the government has introduced reforms to attract foreign investment. Foreign investment has increased over time, but corruption, civil disorder, and occasional international economic sanctions have acted as major disincentives to investment. According to World Bank figures, foreign direct investment (FDI) in Pakistan increased from US$23 million in 1970 to US$612 million in 2003 (approximately 1 percent of the 2003 FDI in China). From 2000 to 2003, FDI increased in finance, transport, communications, mining, quarrying, oil, and gas, with the principal sources being Switzerland, the United States, the United Arab Emirates, and the United Kingdom.

Foreign Aid: The economy is heavily dependent on bilateral and multilateral aid, which substantially influence economic growth. Aid flows have been reduced as a result of international sanctions for Pakistan's suspected support of insurgents in Kashmir and for the country's 1998 nuclear tests. However, after September 11, 2001, the United States and other countries dropped economic sanctions against Pakistan because of its potential role in the war on terrorism. Prior to 2000, Pakistan had never completed an International Monetary Fund (IMF) lending program because of government unwillingness to comply with loan package conditions and political issues such as nuclear weapons tests or difficulties in Kashmir. However, from 2000 to 2004 Pakistan's relations with the IMF showed marked improvement.

Currency and Exchange Rate: For decades Pakistan's official currency, the rupee (Rs), has declined in value against the U.S. dollar. The official exchange rate was Rs4.76 to US$1 in 1970, Rs9.85 to US$1 in 1980, Rs21.61 to US$1 in 1990, Rs53.65 to US$1 in 2000, and approximately Rs59.34 to US$1 in late February 2005.

Fiscal Year: July 1 to June 30.

TRANSPORTATION AND TELECOMMUNICATIONS

Overview: Pakistan's transportation infrastructure has suffered from government neglect. Although there are some signs of improvement, foreign observers often contend that the poor transportation infrastructure inhibits economic growth potential. Both the quality and quantity of government-funded rail and bus service have declined, and in some cases operations have ceased altogether. As a result, private buses, taxis, autorickshaws, and horse-drawn tongas meet most urban transportation demand. These vehicles are unregulated, and safety issues abound. Various government programs have attempted to improve transportation through highway construction and automobile imports, but these endeavors have been costly, and highway capacity is substantially underutilized. Statistics show an increase in freight and passenger traffic on roads, but the increase is believed to be due to the declining quality of rail service rather than to the increasing affordability of automobiles. Studies cite significant, accompanying problems with vehicular pollution, increasing traffic density, and high numbers of traffic fatalities.

By contrast, Pakistan's telecommunications infrastructure has fared somewhat better, although the government's periodic control of communications industries is believed to have limited service improvements. Legislation in 1991 encouraged private-sector participation in communications services by privatizing state-run communications providers and licensing communications provision. However, 1995 legislation granted the publicly traded Pakistan Telecommunication Company Limited (PTCL) a monopoly over telephone services. In 2003 the government announced that telecommunications would be deregulated, yet the results of this change were not yet apparent by early 2005.

Roads: Roads, road traffic, and motor vehicles all have increased substantially since the early 1990s. According to government statistics, from 1994 to 2003 total road length increased from 196,877 to 251,845 kilometers, and highways increased, from 104,001 to 151,028 kilometers. The total number of registered motor vehicles also increased from 3.5 million to 5.2 million, including 2.5 million motorcycles, 1.3 million automobiles, and 178,000 trucks. In the early 1990s, the government announced plans to shift passenger and freight traffic from roads to rail, but by 2004 the declining quality and quantity of rail service continued to prompt increases in private and commercial use of roads.

Railroads: The railroad system is publicly owned, but government funding has been insufficient to maintain the system. Government figures indicate that operating revenues exceeded operating expenses from FY 1994 to FY 2003, but the deterioration in the quantity and quality of service suggests that major problems persist. From 1994 to 2003, the quantity of track kilometers fell from 8,775 to 7,791 kilometers, and route kilometers dropped from 12,625 to 11,515 kilometers. Of the track kilometers, 7,346 kilometers were 1.676-millimeter gauge, and 445 kilometers were 1.000-millimeter gauge. Passenger journeys peaked at 85 million in FY 1989 and declined until FY 1999, after which they increased to 72.4 million in FY 2003. Freight tonnage fell from 8 million tons in FY 1994 to 6.2 million tons in FY 2003. In the same period, the number of locomotives decreased from 676 to 577, and the quantity of coaches fell from 2,831 to 1,843.

Since 1992, various privatization ventures have been terminated and placed back on the market, and the federal government has attempted to transfer responsibility for some rail services to local and provincial authorities. Urban and suburban passenger rail service is often irregular and slower than road transport, but the government plans to build passenger rail systems in Karachi, Lahore, Islamabad, and Rawalpindi. A proposed rail line connecting Pakistan with Iran has been stalled because of a lack of funding.

Ports: According to government statistics, the tonnage handled by ports increased from 30 million tons in FY 1994 to 41.2 million tons in FY 2003. In the same period, the number of twenty-foot-equivalent-units (TEUs) increased from 409,670 to 615,826. In 2004 Pakistan had two ports, Karachi and Port Qasim, both of which were upgraded in the 1990s. Karachi handles approximately 60 percent of import and export cargo and is linked by a daily container train to an inland terminal at Lahore. Port Qasim handles about 40 percent of import and export cargo. The first phase of a multipurpose port located at Gwadar on the Balochistan coast was expected to be operational in early 2005, with a second phase still under construction. A deepwater port at Keti Bandar, 100 kilometers southeast of Karachi, is planned as part of a private power project.

Inland and Coastal Waterways: Inland water transport basically has been nonexistent since the nineteenth century, although there have been government proposals to change this situation. Bridges, irrigation systems, and seasonal changes in water availability limit tremendously the navigability of former inland waterways, particularly the Indus River system. There is small-scale use between Sukkur and Kalabagh on the Indus River, and Pakistani government and transportation analysts have considered inland water routes linking Port Qasim with points on the Indus. However, the technical feasibility of these proposals is doubtful, and high capital costs limit their economic feasibility.

Civil Aviation and Airports: Since the 1980s, the air network has expanded. Pakistan has 50 airports with permanently surfaced runways. Karachi, Lahore, Peshawar, Quetta, and Rawalpindi handle both international passenger and cargo flights, and Multan and Turbat handle international cargo. The airports in Karachi and Lahore have expanded their facilities since 1994. From FY 1994 to FY 2003, international passengers increased from 4.1 million to 5.1 million, and international cargo increased slightly from 1.1 million tons to 1.2 million tons. In the same time period, however, domestic passengers declined from 9.1 million to 5.5 million, and domestic cargo fell from 243,000 tons to 187,000 tons. The major international airline is government-owned Pakistan International Airlines, and four other private airlines offer international passenger and cargo services. Pakistan International Airlines flights to New Delhi beginning in January 2004 have been viewed as a sign of improved relations between India and Pakistan.

Pipelines: In 2004 Pakistan had 9,945 kilometers of gas pipelines and 1,821 kilometers of oil pipelines. The government currently is considering several proposed gas pipelines linking Pakistan with Afghanistan, India, Iran, Turkmenistan, and others. As of early 2005, these proposals were still under consideration, at least partly because their proposed routes would go through areas of periodic civil unrest.

Telecommunications: From 1991 to 2002, the estimated number of radios increased only slightly from 10 to 10.2 million, and the estimated number of televisions was unchanged at 2.1 million. The government runs both Azad Kashmir Radio, with three stations, and Pakistan

Broadcasting Corporation, with 35 stations. Three private radio stations also are in operation. Government-run Pakistan Television Corporation maintains four domestic television channels, and there are three private television broadcasters. Foreign channels are available by satellite and cable. Domestic phone service is poor. In the early 2000s, Pakistan had approximately 3.7 million telephones, 8 million cellular telephones, 600,000 personal computers, and 500,000 Internet users.

GOVERNMENT AND POLITICS

Government Overview: The government is based on the much-amended constitution of 1973, which was suspended twice (in 1977 and 1999) and reinstated twice (in 1985 and 2002). According to the constitution, Pakistan is a federal parliamentary system with a president as head of state and a prime minister as head of government. The legislature, or parliament, is the Majlis-i-Shoora (Council of Advisers), consisting of the Lower House, which is often called the National Assembly, and the Upper House, or Senate. National Assembly members are directly elected for five-year terms. Senate members are elected by provincial assemblies, with equal representation from each of the four provinces as well as representatives from the Federally Administered Tribal Areas and Islamabad Capital Territory. Both the Senate and National Assembly may initiate and pass legislation, but only the National Assembly can approve federal budgets and finance bills. However, parliament often has had little real political power. For example, in 2003 the only bill passed by the National Assembly was the national budget.

Executive power lies with the prime minister and president. The prime minister is an elected member of the National Assembly and is the leader of the National Assembly's dominant party or coalition. However, the prime minister also is appointed formally by the president. The prime minister is assisted by a cabinet of ministers who are appointed by the president on the prime minister's advice. An electoral college composed of members of the national and provincial legislatures elects the president for a five-year term, and no individual may hold the office for more than two consecutive terms. By law the president must be a Muslim. The president acts on the advice of the prime minister but has the power to prevent passage of non-finance bills and may dissolve the National Assembly if he concludes that the government cannot operate according to the constitution. The Senate, however, cannot be suspended.

Politics in Pakistan often have not operated according to the constitution. The military and Civil Service of Pakistan (CSP) frequently have been the preeminent actors in the country's power structure, and in 1999 General Pervez Musharraf assumed power in a military coup. Moreover, there has been some concern that Pakistan could become a "failed state" because of the apparent inability of any single entity to control the country, the weakened productivity of a population beset by years of economic difficulties, and continuing problems of communal conflict and terrorism. Ethnic and provincial tensions often are manifested in rivalries between political parties, and several governments have been ended by assassination or military coup rather than by formal, electoral change.

Religion has played an important role in politics, and religious differences have been very salient in Pakistani government and civil society. The government has consistently been faced with tensions of whether and how to synthesize Islamic principles into an essentially secular and Western form of government. Religious differences among politically influential actors have become increasingly prominent since the early 1980s, when politics became more religiously oriented under the rule of General Zia ul-Haq (1977–88). As religious groups' access to government resources increased, groups competed for political resources and the capacity to promote their approach to Islam, and sectarian divisions often became violent.

Administrative Divisions: Pakistan has four provinces—Balochistan, North-West Frontier Province, Punjab, and Sindh—and numerous federally administered areas. Provincial boundaries correspond with areas of numerically dominant linguistic groups, and provinces are divided into a total of 26 divisions that are further subdivided into 101 districts. Federally administered areas include the capital (Islamabad) and 13 Federally Administered Tribal Areas (FATAs) as well as the western third of Jammu and Kashmir, although Kashmir's status is contested by India.

Provincial and Local Government: Each province has a governor appointed by the president, and provinces also have an elected legislative assembly and a chief minister who is the leader of the legislative assembly's majority party or coalition. The chief minister is assisted by a council of ministers chosen by the chief minister and formally approved by the governor. Federally administered areas also have their own legislative entities, which have had less autonomy from the federal government than provincial legislatures. However, tribal areas in the west have traditional legal systems that operate independently of the federal government. Various regimes have promoted local-level Basic Democracies so that communities can have input into federal policy, but these entities have suffered from inconsistent federal government support.

Although provinces and federally administered areas have their own political and administrative institutions, federal government agencies are heavily involved in the affairs of these areas. There are some matters over which both federal and provincial governments can make laws and establish departments for their execution. For example, provincial governments administer agricultural and social services, but the federal government legislates on these matters, and federal agencies also are involved in their administration. Moreover, the federal government has the power to dismiss provincial chief ministers and legislatures.

Judicial and Legal System: The legal system is derived from English common law and is based on the much-amended 1973 constitution and Islamic law (sharia). The Supreme Court, provincial high courts, and other courts have jurisdiction over criminal and civil issues. The president appoints the Supreme Court's chief justice and formally approves other Supreme Court justices as well as provincial high court judges on the advice of the chief justice. The Supreme Court has original, appellate, and advisory jurisdiction, and high courts have original and appellate jurisdiction. The Federal Shariat Court determines whether laws are consistent with Islamic injunctions. Special courts and tribunals hear particular types of cases, such as drugs, commerce, and terrorism. Pakistan's penal code has limited jurisdiction in tribal areas, where law is largely derived from tribal customs.

The 1973 constitution guarantees freedom of speech, press, and religion as well as the right to bail, counsel, habeas corpus, representation, appeal, and numerous other protections. However, the government has constitutional authority to limit civil liberties in accordance with Islamic doctrine, national security, and other circumstances. Pakistani courts can impose the death penalty, and some crimes are punishable by stoning, lashing, or amputation, although these punishments rarely occur outside of tribal areas. The judiciary has limited independence from the executive branch, and the legislative and executive branches often attempt to remove themselves from judicial oversight. The judiciary also suffers from low public credibility, large case backlogs, corruption, and a lack of resources. In 2001, however, the Asian Development Bank pledged US$350 million for judicial reform and improved governance.

Electoral System: Pakistan has universal adult suffrage, and those 18 years of age and older are eligible to vote. As of early 2005, there were 72 million registered voters. The minimum age of candidates is 25 years of age for national and provincial assemblies, 30 for the Senate, and 45 for president. The president sets election dates, and the Election Commission (EC) conducts national and provincial assembly elections, but the EC's chair, the chief election commissioner, oversees elections for local governments, the Senate, and the presidency. The EC is an independent, financially autonomous body, but it has been criticized as having little power to enforce codes of conduct on political parties and candidates. Constituencies are demarcated by population, administrative boundaries, and other factors. In 2002 there were 357 constituencies for the National Assembly and 728 constituencies for provincial assemblies. Sixty seats in the National Assembly and 128 in the provincial assemblies are reserved for women. In addition, 10 seats in the National Assembly and 23 in the provincial assemblies are reserved for non-Muslims. In April 2002, Musharraf's term as president was extended for five years in a national referendum. Elections were held for the national and provincial assemblies in October 2002 and for the Senate in February 2003. However, domestic and international observers have criticized these and earlier elections as flawed.

Politics and Political Parties: Political parties have increased in number but declined in political power, particularly in relation to the military. Since the late 1990s, numerous parties have splintered into factions, dividing electoral support and leading to the formation of coalitions that often also dissolve into factions. The three parties with the greatest electoral support since 1988 all have become shadows of their former selves. The Pakistan People's Party (PPP) and Pakistan Muslim League-Nawaz Sharif (PML-N) have splintered into numerous parties, and the Muttahida Quami Movement (MQM) has lost substantial legitimacy as a result of involvement in violence. Officially, 73 parties contested the 2002 National Assembly elections, but only 3 percent of voters were registered as members of a political party. As a result of elections in 2002, a coalition led by the Pakistan Muslim League-Quaid-e-Azam (PML-Q) assumed control of provincial assemblies in Punjab and Sindh and the National Assembly. This party has been closely associated with the government of General Musharraf. Parties often have no constitutions, membership lists, or documentation of funding sources. Furthermore, electoral support is rarely nationwide and most often is drawn from particular religious, ethnic, or regional bases. The military has given financial support to religious parties as a counterweight to secular parties, but electoral support for religious parties has been well below 10 percent nationwide. Many parties have separate wings for women and youth, and many are accused of having militias that collect funds and intimidate opponents.

Mass Media: In the early twenty-first century, the amount of print media in Pakistan declined precipitously while total circulation increased. From 1994 to 1997, the total number of daily, monthly, and other publications increased from 3,242 to 4,455 but had dropped to just 945 by 2003 with most of the decline occurring in Punjab Province. However, from 1994 to 2003 total print circulation increased substantially, particularly for dailies (3 million to 6.2 million). Print media are published in 11 languages, but most are published in Urdu and Sindhi, and English-language publications are numerous. The press generally publishes free from censorship and has played an active role in national elections, but journalists often exercise self-censorship as a result of arrests and intimidation by government and societal actors. Most print media are privately owned, but the government controls the National Press Trust, a major newspaper publisher, and the Associated Press of Pakistan, one of the two major news agencies. The constitution guarantees the rights of free speech and press but also allows for government restrictions in cases of offenses against Islam, public morality, national security, and other circumstances. In fact, the government can fine and imprison those who broadcast material that is deemed inconsistent with "national and social values."

Foreign Relations: Pakistan's primary foreign policy objectives are protection from external threats and the preservation of territorial integrity. Foreign alliances often have been based on mutual—and sometimes ephemeral—strategic interests. Contentious relations with India dominate foreign relations and are largely due to perennial tensions over Kashmir, which was the basis of wars in 1948, 1965, 1971, and 1999. Various talks in 2003–5 have eased tensions but not mutual suspicions. China has perhaps been Pakistan's most consistent ally because of shared antipathies of other countries, such as India and Russia, but in the 1990s China assumed a more distant relationship as a result of India's growing military prowess, Russia's military decline, and other factors. However, China is alleged to have supplied Pakistan with nuclear weapons material, ostensibly to counter India's nuclear weapons. Relations with Afghanistan have been harmonious and tense, often simultaneously. The two countries have a disputed border, but Pakistan supported insurgents in Afghanistan against Soviet occupation in the 1980s and was a key ally of the Taliban in the 1990s. Since their 1971 war, Pakistan and Bangladesh typically have had close ties based largely on shared opposition to India. Relations with Islamic Middle Eastern countries generally have been close, but ties with largely Shia Iran have been strained.

For countries outside South Asia and the Middle East, relations generally are based on Pakistan's perceived strategic value in the international system. Pakistan's successful nuclear tests in 1998 initially led to international sanctions that were later eased as a result of concerns that an economically weakened Pakistan might provide nuclear material to other nations. After September 11, 2001, the United States and other countries saw Pakistan as an important ally in fighting international terrorists operating in Afghanistan, and international aid increased substantially. Pakistan's relations with the United States have resumed the closeness of the 1980s. However, Pakistan's improved relations with the United States have had important ramifications for the government's domestic support, particularly among some religious parties who perceive the government as acting against Islamic injunctions.

Membership in International Organizations: Pakistan is an active participant in international organizations, although its membership in the British Commonwealth of Nations was suspended from 1999 to 2004 because of the military coup. Pakistan views international organizations as a means of addressing the actions of relatively stronger countries and often appeals to international organizations such as the United Nations (UN) on matters such as Kashmir.

Pakistan's international memberships include: the Asian Development Bank, Colombo Plan, Economic Cooperation Organization, Food and Agriculture Organization of the United Nations, Group of 24, Group of 77, International Atomic Energy Agency, International Bank for Reconstruction and Development, International Chamber of Commerce, International Civil Aviation Organization, International Confederation of Free Trade Unions, International Criminal Police Organization, International Development Association, Islamic Development Bank, International Finance Corporation, International Federation of Red Cross and Red Crescent Societies, International Fund for Agricultural Development, International Hydrographic Organization, International Labour Organization, International Maritime Organization, International Monetary Fund, International Olympic Committee, International Organization for Migration, International Organization for Standardization, International Telecommunication Union, Nonaligned Movement, Organisation for the Prohibition of Chemical Weapons, Organization of American States (observer), Organization of the Islamic Conference, Permanent Court of Arbitration, South Asian Association for Regional Cooperation, UN, UN Conference on Trade and Development, UN Educational, Scientific and Cultural Organization, UN High Commissioner for Refugees, UN Industrial Development Organization, UN Institute for Training and Research, UN Security Council (temporary), Universal Postal Union, World Confederation of Labor, World Customs Organization, World Federation of Trade Unions, World Health Organization, World Intellectual Property Organization, World Meteorological Organization, World Tourism Organization, and World Trade Organization.

Major International Treaties: Pakistan is a signatory to various international treaties including: the Basel Convention on the Control of Transboundary Movements of Hazardous Substances, Biological and Toxin Weapons Convention, Chemical Weapons Convention, Convention on Biological Diversity, Convention on International Trade in Endangered Species of Wild Flora and Fauna, Convention on the Physical Protection of Nuclear Material, Convention on the Prevention of Marine Pollution by Dumping Wastes and Other Matter, Convention on the Prohibition of Military or Any Other Hostile Use of Environmental Modification Techniques, Convention on Wetlands of International Importance Especially as Waterfowl Habitat, International Plant Protection Convention, Kyoto Protocol to the United Nations (UN) Framework Convention on Climate Change, Montreal Protocol on Substances that Deplete the Ozone Layer, Nuclear Safety Convention, Protocol of 1978 Relating to the International Convention for the Prevention of Pollution from Ships, UN Convention on the Law of the Sea, UN Convention to Combat Desertification, UN Framework Convention on Climate Change, and Vienna Convention for the Protection of the Ozone Layer.

Pakistan has signed but not ratified the Convention on Fishing and Conservation of Living Resources of the High Seas. It is not a party to either the Treaty on the Non-Proliferation of Nuclear Weapons (NPT) or the Missile Technology Control Regime (MTCR). Pakistan has argued that the NPT and MTCR are not relevant to the country's security concerns because they do not reduce nuclear weapons proliferation by states already possessing nuclear weapons, and they deny non-nuclear states the right to have nuclear weapons.

NATIONAL SECURITY

Armed Forces Overview: The military is formally called the Pakistan Armed Forces, and as of 2004 consisted of approximately 619,000 active personnel in the army (550,000), air force (45,000), and navy (24,000), as well as 513,000 reserves. Under the 1973 constitution, the federal government controls the armed forces, and the president is the commander in chief. The Ministry of Defence has a permanent staff of civil servants headed by the defense secretary general, and the minister of defense is a civilian member of the prime minister's cabinet. The Joint Chiefs of Staff Committee deals with problems concerning military aspects of state security and is charged with integrating and coordinating the army, navy, and air force. The committee's secretariat acts as the principal link between the service headquarters and the Ministry of Defence. The Directorate for Inter-Services Intelligence (ISI) is of particular importance at the joint services level because it manages covert operations outside of Pakistan (and in internationally disputed areas) and because it has been involved in domestic politics, usually to keep track of the incumbent regime's opponents. The chief of the army staff (COAS) is the key power holder in the armed forces and is also one of the triumvirate that runs the country, along with the prime minister and president. The COAS usually operates from army headquarters in Rawalpindi. General Pervez Musharraf acts as both president and COAS. Musharraf also heads a National Security Council composed of politicians and senior military officers.

Under the constitution, the military is responsible for defending the nation against external aggression and threats of war and is to aid civil authorities only when called to do so. The military is forbidden constitutionally from acting independently of the elected political leadership in domestic matters. However, from 1947 to 2004 military generals have acted as head of state for nearly 30 years, and in times of civilian government the armed forces have routinely intervened on domestic and foreign policy issues. The military justifies its consistent involvement in politics as protection from malign foreign interests and corrupt and incompetent politicians. Although public opinion surveys are rare, it appears that the public dislikes military rule, yet consistently has a more favorable view of the military than of elected officials.

Because the military conducts its affairs with carefully defended secrecy, the degree to which army officers and personnel are religiously motivated is debated. However, Western analysts tend to conclude that whereas the military increasingly sees itself as serving Islam, the institution's decision making is still largely secular. Military intervention in politics is designed to limit civilian involvement in sensitive matters, such as Kashmir, nuclear disarmament, internal military personnel decisions, and defense spending. The military also is extensively involved in the economy, and military enterprises produce approximately 3 percent of the gross national product. Military enterprises include the Army Welfare Trust (AWT), whose assets include the Askari Bank, one of the country's largest financial institutions, and the Fauji Foundation, which is the country's biggest conglomerate. These and other military financial institutions often are exempt from taxes and regulations covering the manufacturing sector and asset disclosure.

With regard to military strategy, the military's budget and personnel have reduced strategy to largely defensive objectives, such as limited offensive tactics in bordering areas (particularly Kashmir), use of irregular forces, and deterring and countering possible attacks from foreign powers (particularly India). The military's history of far lower military expenditures and capabilities than India has prompted the military to attempt to impose high costs on India to force its withdrawal from Kashmir. Furthermore, the military hopes that its nuclear capabilities can reduce the disadvantages of its conventional forces. However, the theoretical deterrence between nuclear powers has not limited military engagement between India and Pakistan—as exemplified by the 1999 Kargil War—and analysts believe that Pakistan's military strategy historically has suffered from overly optimistic assessments of potential success and underestimations of diplomatic and military losses, as well as a lack of contingency planning.

Foreign Military Relations: Pakistan has sought to become an important actor in international politics, but its foreign military alliances often are intended to address matters with bordering countries. Other countries have established alliances with Pakistan to address their own strategic interests in South and Central Asia, and these alliances have tended to be ephemeral. Pakistan's military relationship with China started in the 1970s as a way of countering India, but China has softened its relations since India's military strength has increased. Still, Pakistan and China maintain a military relationship, including periodic joint military exercises. United States aid in the 1980s was significantly reduced after the Soviet Union pulled out of Afghanistan in 1989 but resumed after the September 11, 2001, terrorist attacks. Moreover, in March 2004 the United States granted Pakistan status as a major non-North Atlantic Treaty Organization ally, which provides access to U.S. military equipment and cooperation. In fact, the United States is one of the largest suppliers of military equipment to Pakistan along with China and Russia. Pakistan's military relations with India have been contentious, and the two countries fought a limited conflict in Kashmir in 1999. However, under the 1999 Lahore Agreement the two countries provide each other with advance notification of missile tests, and in 2003 and 2004 they engaged in several high-level discussions that have eased tensions.

External Threat: The military and public generally view India as the nation's primary security threat, and opposition to India is often a greater source of social cohesion than either Islam or Urdu. India's far greater military capabilities have been a source of both fear and frustration, and many suspect that this imbalance has prompted Pakistan to engage Indian forces indirectly through supporting insurgents morally, financially, or otherwise. Whether Pakistan has done so is debated, but it seems clear that the country's newly demonstrated nuclear capabilities have helped level military differences with its rival neighbor. Yet India is not the country's only security concern, as Pakhtun and Balochi irredentist movements in Pakistan's western provinces have contributed to sometimes-tense relations with neighboring Afghanistan.

Defense Budget: According to World Bank figures for 1988 to 2003, Pakistan's military expenditures represented 25–29 percent of central government expenditures and 6–7 percent of gross national income. In fiscal year (FY) 2004, military expenditures constituted 18 percent of government expenditures. Historically, Pakistan's governments have used defense spending to stimulate economic growth.

Major Military Units: The army, with 550,000 active personnel and 500,000 reserves, is organized into nine corps located at Bahawalpur, Gujranwala, Karachi, Lahore, Mangla, Multan, Peshawar, Quetta, and Rawalpindi. The Northern Area Command is headquartered at Gilgit and is directly responsible to army general headquarters. The army has 2 armored divisions, 19 infantry divisions including 1 area command, 9 corps artillery brigades, 26 independent brigades

(7 armored, 1 mechanized, 6 infantry, 5 artillery, and 7 engineer), 3 armored reconnaissance regiments, 1 special forces group, and 1 air defense command. The navy has 24,000 active personnel—including 1,400 marines and 2,000 in the Maritime Security Agency—and 5,000 reserves. The navy has four commands: fleet, logistics, naval installations in the north of Pakistan, and fleet headquarters at Karachi, the nation's only major naval base. Two bases are under construction at Gwadar and Ormara. The air force has 45,000 active personnel and 8,000 reserves. Air force headquarters in Rawalpindi has directorates for operations, electronics, administration, and maintenance. The air force has three regional air commands: Northern (in Peshawar), Central (Sargodha), and Southern (Faisal).

Major Military Equipment: In 2004 the army had an estimated 2,461 tanks, 1,146 armored personnel carriers, 1,829 tube-launched optically-tracked wire-guided "TOW" missiles, 260 self-propelled artillery, 52 multiple rocket launchers, 2,350 mortars, 165 surface-to-surface missiles, 10,500 antitank guided weapons, and 1,900 air defense guns. The army also had 80 observation aircraft, 45 liaison aircraft, 2 survey aircraft, 22 attack helicopters, and 131 transport helicopters. The navy had 8 anti-surface warfare submarines, 3 inshore submarines, 7 frigates, 6 missile craft, 3 coastal patrol craft, 6 combat aircraft, and 9 armed helicopters. The air force had 415 combat aircraft and no armed helicopters. Pakistan became a nuclear state in 1998 and periodically tests nuclear-capable short- and medium-range missiles.

Military Service: Military service is voluntary, and active-service personnel are liable for duty eight years after active service ends. Officers are obligated to serve until 50 years of age, other ranks until 45 years of age. Women serve in the military but are a numerical minority.

Paramilitary Forces: The central government (specifically the Ministry of Interior) controls the coast guard, paramilitary forces, and numerous specialized police agencies, such as the Federal Investigative Agency and railroad and airport police forces. However, provincial governments organize paramilitary forces, which often act as an extension of the army to assist provincial police in internal security matters. In addition, senior government officials often have strong control over security forces and have at times established personal security forces. The largest paramilitary organization is the 185,000-member National Guard, which comprises the National Cadet Corps, the Women Guards, and the Janbaz Force. The Frontier Corps reportedly has 65,000 members and is responsible for Balochistan and the North-West Frontier Province. The Pakistan Rangers has 35,000 to 40,000 members and deals with unrest in Punjab. The Northern Light Infantry has an estimated 12,000 members, and the Maritime Security Agency, which is under the navy's direction, has an estimated 2,000 personnel.

Foreign Military Forces: Pakistan hosts 45 military observers from nine countries stationed in Jammu and Kashmir under the United Nations Military Observer Group in India and Pakistan (UNMOGIP). U.S. military forces occasionally work with Pakistan's military against insurgents supporting the Taliban and al Qaeda in areas of Pakistan bordering Afghanistan.

Military Forces Abroad: In 2004 Pakistan's military participated in United Nations peacekeeping missions in Burundi, Côte d'Ivoire (9 personnel including 3 observers), the Democratic Republic of the Congo (1,092 personnel including 26 observers), East Timor (78 personnel including 5 observers), Georgia (8 observers), Liberia (2,762 personnel including 16 observers), Sierra Leone (3,865 personnel including 15 observers), Serbia and Montenegro (1 observer), and Western Sahara (7 observers).

Police: Provincial governments are charged with police administration in their respective jurisdictions, and provincial police forces operate independently. The federal government is largely uninvolved in provincial police administration but controls police in federally administered and tribal areas. The federal minister of interior supervises police nationwide, and the Police Service of Pakistan (PSP) selects, trains, and assigns senior officers to provincial or central government agencies. Although service in the PSP is competitive and well paid, lower-ranking police personnel often have far lower education, skills, and motivation. Police often are accused of routine extortion, violating civil liberties, and acting to preserve the tenure of government officials rather than the rule of law. The quantity of overall crime and various types of crime (such as murder and banditry) increased steadily from 1992 to 2003, and the extensive availability and use of automatic weapons in Pakistani society is often referred to as the "Kalashnikov Culture." Furthermore, the population generally does not perceive the police to be effective against crime or publicly accountable.

Internal Security and Terrorism: Pakistan has numerous categories of terrorism and internal threats, with most insurgent groups identifying themselves as religious or ethnic separatists. Some political parties represent distinct religious and ethnic communities, and rivalries among these parties have been violent. Violence between religiously identified groups is rarely based solely on differing religious doctrines but rather the different social, political, and economic statuses that correlate with religion. Some Islamic militias have connections to the Taliban and al Qaeda, which was linked to two assassination attempts on President Musharraf in December 2003. Militant organizations have some influence on Pakistan's foreign policy, and militants in Pakistan (such as Harkat-ul-Ansar) have assisted militant organizations in countries whose governments are perceived as oppressing Muslims. There are also concerns that Pakistan's nuclear arsenal could be seized by insurgents in an event such as a coup or assassination of the nation's president. However, the government claims that it has enacted security measures to prevent such a threat and that the numerical and political superiority of religious moderates over religious extremists is a substantial obstacle to the latter's access to Pakistan's nuclear weapons.

The most significant violence between religious groups is between Islamic militias, the Shia militia Sipah-e-Mohammed Pakistan (SMP, "Army of Mohammed") and the Sunni militias Sipah-e-Sahaba Pakistan (SSP, "Army of the Friends of the Prophet") and Lashkar-e-Jhangvi (LeJ, "Army of Jhangvi"). The violence has, at times, disrupted both civil order and the economies in areas of Sindh and Punjab provinces. The violence has resulted in large part from the influx of weapons and returning mujahideen from Afghanistan, as well as financial support from large landowners, drug lords, and some political parties. Tensions between ethnic groups often stem from perceptions that other ethnic groups dominate politics and economics to the detriment of minority ethnicities. The Muhajir Quami Movement (MQM) was involved in substantial conflict in the 1980s and early 1990s but has since been far more quiescent as a result of internal factionalism and an apparent lack of motivating doctrine. The only other significant ethnic violence involves secessionists in Balochistan, who contend that the government is appropriating the province's mineral wealth while providing little economic benefit in return.

There are also long-suspected connections of foreign-sponsored subversion, such as Indian support of Sindhi dissidents and Iranian ties to Shia and Balochi militants.

Human Rights: The government's human rights record is generally regarded as poor by domestic and international observers, although there have been some improvements since 2000. Security forces use excessive and sometimes lethal force and are complicit in extrajudicial killings of civilians and suspected militants. The police and military have been accused of engaging in physical abuse, rape, and arbitrary arrest and detention, particularly in areas of acute conflict. Although the government has enacted measures to counter these problems, abuses continue. Furthermore, courts suffer from lack of funds, outside intervention, and deep case backlogs that lead to long trial delays and lengthy pretrial detentions. Many observers inside and outside Pakistan contend that Pakistan's legal code is largely concerned with crime, national security, and domestic tranquility and less with the protection of individual rights. Provincial and local governments have arrested journalists and closed newspapers that report on matters perceived as socially offensive or critical of the government. Journalists also have been victims of violence and intimidation by various groups and individuals. In spite of these difficulties, the press publishes freely, although journalists often exercise self-restraint in their writing. In 2002 citizens participated in elections for the National Assembly, but those elections were criticized as deeply flawed by domestic and international observers.

Societal actors also are responsible for human rights abuses. Violence by drug lords and sectarian militias claims numerous innocent lives, discrimination and violence against women are widespread, human trafficking is problematic, and debt slavery and bonded labor persist. The government often ignores abuses against children and religious minorities, and government institutions and some Muslim groups have persecuted non-Muslims and used some laws as the legal basis for doing so. The Blasphemy Law, for example, allows life imprisonment or the death penalty for contravening Islamic principles, but legislation was passed in October 2004 to eliminate misuse of the law. Furthermore, the social acceptance of many these problems hinders their eradication. One prominent example is honor killings ("karo kari"), which are believed to have accounted for more than 4,000 deaths from 1998 to 2003. Many view this practice as indicative of a feudal mentality and as an anathema to Islam, but others defend the practice as a means of punishing violators of cultural norms and view attempts to stop it to as an assault on cultural heritage.